Sabbath Is My Favorite Day

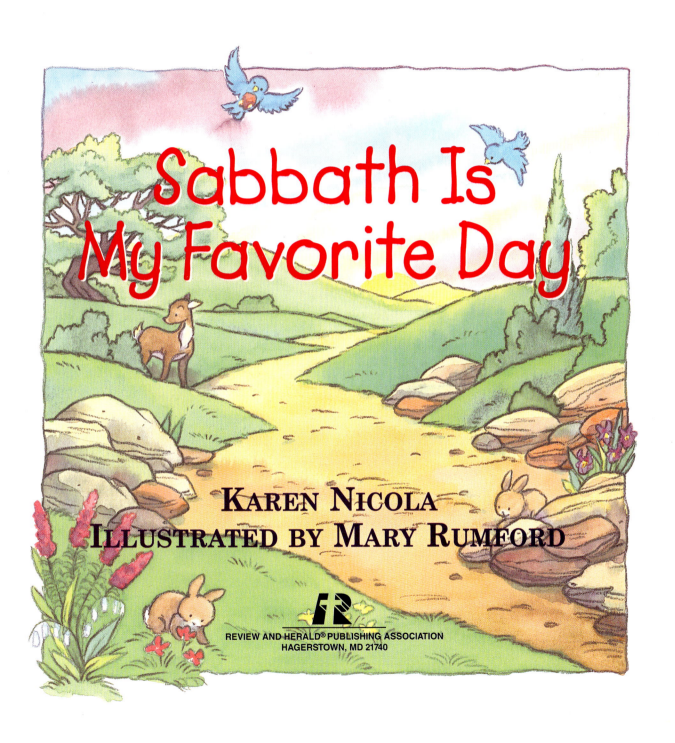

Copyright © 1995 by
Review and Herald® Publishing Association

The author assumes full responsibility
for the accuracy of all facts and quotations as cited in this book.

Scripture credited to ICB are quoted from the *International Children's Bible, New Century Version,* copyright © 1983, 1986, 1988 by Word Publishing, Dallas, Texas 75039. Used by permission.

This book was
Edited by Gerald Wheeler
Designed by Patricia S. Wegh
Illustrations by Mary Rumford
Typeset: 15/19 Century Schoolbook

PRINTED IN U.S.A.

04 03 02 01 00   5 4 3 2

R&H Cataloging Service
Nicola, Karen
    Sabbath is my favorite day.

    1. Sabbath—Juvenile works. I. Title.

        263.2

ISBN 0-8280-0727-6

Austin

Hi, I'm Austin. I'm 3½ years old. I learn new things every day. Now I am learning about Sabbath. I like Sabbath. It's my favorite day.

My dad says that Sabbath is one of God's presents to me. I didn't understand what he meant at first. But Dad helped me to understand.

Dad said that it took God six days to make everything. God made the sky, the flowers, animals, fish, waterfalls, birds, and people. Then God made a special day that was like a birthday. I love birthdays! When I heard that, I began to see how I could really love Sabbath.

Dad says that we do not have a cake, candles, and presents each Sabbath. But we have something better. God made a special day for us to be together as a family. That's why Dad doesn't go to work on Sabbath.

God's present to me is time. I don't know how to tell time yet, but I do know when it is time to play. I know when it is time to eat. And I know when it is bedtime. Dad says that the Sabbath time begins when it gets dark on Friday night. Then Sabbath time ends when it gets dark on Saturday night. God is with us in a very special way during that time. It is like when your most favorite person comes to a birthday party.

I'm happy God gave me the Sabbath time to get to know Him better. God must want to get to know me too. Sabbath is my get-to-know-God day. I love Sabbath.

On Friday night my mom makes sure my special Sabbath clothes and shoes are clean for church. I am learning how to help her get my things ready. I can fold my socks after she takes them out of the dryer. I like to clean my shoes. Dad helps me polish them. He puts on the dark color. After it dries, I rub my shoes with a cloth. Then they get shiny.

My mom says that God is the King of the universe (that's the world and all the stars). I am a prince. When I didn't understand what she meant, Mom told me more. She said that a king's child has a special name. A prince is a king's little boy and is very special because his dad is king. Mom told me that I have two dads. One is my daddy in my house. My other dad is God, my heavenly Father. She also told me that a king's little girl is called a princess. I guess that means my sister is a princess. Sometimes, though, she just seems like a sister, not a princess.

    Mom says I dress in my very best clothes when I go to church because I am a prince. We go to church to meet God our heavenly Father, the King of the universe.

    God isn't at church in His body form. He would be too bright for us to look at. Instead God comes in the love and happiness we feel from others when we are at church. He even comes to church in me when I invite Him into my heart. Others know that He has come in me when I smile and am helpful to my Sabbath school teacher.

    I feel special when I'm dressed up and my hair is combed. I like being God's little prince.

Debbie

Hi, I'm Debbie. I'm 5 years old, and I am Austin's sister.

Sabbath is my favorite day. I especially like the part of Sabbath that comes on Friday night. Do you want to know why I like it best? Well, I'll tell you.

When the sun goes down on Friday night, Mom and Dad light all the candles, and I turn out all the lights. Everything seems quiet and peaceful. I love to cuddle up in Daddy's lap. The candles look so pretty. The light from them makes everyone's face seem special and happy.

We sing our favorite songs about Jesus. Then Mom or Dad reads our Sabbath school lesson and other favorite Bible stories. Sometimes we even get to make a long-distance telephone call to our grandparents. We tell them "Happy Sabbath," and they always tell us how much they love us and miss seeing us.

Once I asked Mom why we always lit candles on Friday night when Sabbath started. She told me it was our family tradition. I didn't know what a "tradition" was, so she explained that a tradition is something that a family has done for a long time.

The candle lighting tradition began in Jewish families a long time ago. Every Friday night the mother would fix a special meal and light two special candles. The family would gather around the table and sing a song and recite a Bible verse. The mother would always light the candles. Some Jewish families still do this.

My mother explained that traditions are good when they help us to remember Jesus. But a tradition can be bad when it keeps us from knowing what God is really like.

I think our candlelight tradition helps me remember Jesus and God's special present, the Sabbath.

When we light the candles in our house I remember how Jesus is like light to me.

I also remember how special Sabbath is when we have our special Friday night traditions.

Austin

It's me, Austin. I love to go to Sabbath school! I go to Cradle Roll. Because I am one of the oldest and biggest children there, I help my teachers a lot. It makes me feel good when I help. I know Teacher Dave and Teacher Kathy love me. They always smile and give me a big hug. They hug the other children too. We take turns sitting on their laps during Sabbath School.

I like to sing in Sabbath school. Our teacher gives us bells to sing along with. Sometimes we sing loudly, and sometimes we sing softly. Other times we get to sing and tap sticks. I like the sounds in Sabbath school.

I have special friends in Sabbath school. Jiear is a little baby. I like to sit next to him. His mommy still stays with him. But soon Jiear will be able to go to the felt board by himself. Angela is another friend. Her grandmother brings her. Angela gets to learn about Jesus only in Sabbath school. David, Sally, Antonio, and Katelynn are my other Sabbath school friends.

Teacher Dave tells the Bible story each Sabbath. He lets us help him. We put the felts on the board to make the picture. When I listen carefully to the Bible story I am getting to know God better. Teacher Dave helps me say the words in my memory verse. Then he gives me a special sticker for my *Little Friend* paper.

I bring my offering to Sabbath school. It is fun to put the money in the camel or the little church or the grass hut. My offering helps other boys and girls to learn about Jesus.

Sometimes the littlest children get fussy. Then our teachers take us for a walk outside. We go slowly and stop to see the things God made for us. Then we sing "Here is the way we walk to church," when we come back in.

Sabbath school is a very happy place. I learn about Jesus and God the Father in Sabbath school. They must be happy all the time if I feel this happy when I come to learn about them.

Debbie

This is Debbie again. And I'm going to tell you about some more things I like about Sabbath.

As we drove to church one Sabbath morning, Mom and Dad reminded us that we were going to God's house. Daddy said that God has more than one house to go to every Sabbath morning and that He can be in each of His special houses around the world all at the same time.

"Wow!" I said. "How can God do that?"

Daddy said that God has a special part of Him that is everywhere at the same time. That part is called the Holy Spirit. The Holy Spirit is happy to be with us in church on Sabbath mornings. God also sends His angels to be in our church. When we remember these things, church is very special!

I'm learning to be quiet. Mom says that God's voice is very soft. When we are loud during church, we can't hear His voice. Sometimes we keep others from hearing His voice when we are too noisy. Mom also said that God's voice speaks to our thinking place in our heads. I have heard God's voice during special music. He said "I love you" to my thinking place, and I told Him "I love You too."

When I give my offering during church I feel good to know I can help others with my money. Maybe the angels are putting their wings around me to make me feel happy.

God's house is for both kids and grown-ups. I like the children's story during church the best. During the children's story I can hear things God wants me to know.

Church is such a special place. It is God's special house for all His children to come together to sing, pray, and listen to His voice.

Of all the meals in the week, Sabbath lunch is my favorite! Sometimes we stay for church potluck. Children at least 5 years old get to sit at a special kids' table. I like sitting with my friends.

On other Sabbaths Mommy makes a special lunch and invites some of the old people to come home with us. Mommy says they get very lonely eating all their meals by themselves. Imagine how sad that would feel. So I am extra friendly to the old people to help make them feel happy on Sabbath.

Sometimes in the summer we take a Sabbath picnic up to the mountains. I especially like Sabbath picnics because Mommy and Dad bring nature books so we can learn about the trees, birds, and flowers all around us.

But I like it the best when we go to someone else's home to share Sabbath lunch. When we walk in the door the smells are so good that I feel extra hungry. Mommy says it is a Sabbath tradition to set the table with the nicest plates and glasses. Even cloth napkins! I like being all dressed up and seated with the grown-ups. It makes me feel important.

I remember that Sabbath is God's special gift to me and that I am His princess, and together we are celebrating God's power to create the world and all the nice things in it.

I'm looking forward to telling you about my most happy Sabbath day. But first my brother, Austin, will tell you about his favorite Sabbath.

Austin

My sister Debbie and I have been talking about our favorite day, Sabbath. I want to tell you what I do on Sabbath after lunch.

Sometimes I take a nap.

And sometimes I take a walk with Mommy, Daddy, Debbie, and the dog. We go to the park and down along the creek. When it's hot I get in the water and splash. But when it's cold, we just walk along the edge and listen for different bird sounds. Then we go to the swings, slide, and merry-go-round. When I swing up high in the sky, it feels like I'm flying.

I wonder what kind of playground God is building up in heaven for us kids? My mom told me that God made kids special. God knows just what I am like. He knows what makes me feel the happiest. I can't wait to go to heaven and be with God and all the things He has to make me happy.

Sometimes just Daddy and I go down to the river. It's a big river with lots of rocks. Daddy made a sling like the one David used with Goliath! Daddy slings the rocks across the river. They go so fast, I can't even see them. But I can hear them go z-i-n-g.

I like getting big rocks and throwing them in the water. They go *splash! Cluck!* Then Daddy and I laugh and laugh. When we're at the river, Daddy talks to me about his best friend, Jesus. Daddy will tell me Bible stories. He says that I am his special son and he loves me very much. Often we just sit quietly next to each other. Sometimes he lifts me high and carries me on his shoulders.

I am so happy God gave me Sabbath. I get to be with my daddy on Sabbath, and I like that a lot.

Debbie

Debbie here, and I'm going to tell you about my favorite Sabbath.

My fifth birthday came on Sabbath. Isn't that great? I thought it was wonderful because we could celebrate two birthdays at the same time—mine and the world's.

When I went to Sabbath school, my teacher asked me to come up front. Everyone sang to me while I put my birthday money in a special box. My teacher gave me a new Sabbath coloring book. After church, some of the grown-ups even wished me "Happy Birthday."

Because it was my birthday, my mom and dad invited another family with children to come over for lunch and then "something special." We ate my favorite food—spaghetti.

Then it was time for "something special." I didn't know what it was. Nobody else did either, except Mom. But she explained that we were going on a Sabbath "treasure hunt." She told us how to find the first clue that would give us directions.

The directions told us to follow the trail until we found another little blue paper all rolled up. The little blue paper told us where to find the "treasure."

When we finally found it, the "treasure" was a Bible hidden behind a tree with a card for Megan, my friend. She read her card and the Bible verse that she was to look up. It said, "Remember the Lord in everything you do. And he will give you success" (Prov. 3:6, ICB). Then the card gave directions to find the next "hidden treasure." My mom had a "hidden treasure" for everyone who went on the treasure hunt, even the grown-ups.

I was really happy that Sabbath birthday! I don't think I'll ever forget it. Not ever!

Now I want to tell you of some of the other fun things we do on Sabbath.

When it's nice weather, we go to the park and play nature object lesson. Dad makes up a list of things for us to find like rocks, sticks, weeds, flowers, and berries. After we've found them, we sit in a circle and tell how they remind us of Jesus.

I like to learn about the birds, trees, and flowers on Sabbath. God made all these things for us to enjoy and explore. Mom says that nature is God's second book. His first book is the Bible. We learn about God from the Bible in Sabbath school and church. In the afternoon we learn about God through the things He created in nature.

God takes care of all His creatures. The Bible says that He knows when even the smallest bird dies. God makes beautiful colors in the flowers. He must like colors. God makes the birds each have a different sound. He must like music. And He makes trees grow big and strong. God is big and strong like trees.

Sometimes on rainy Sabbaths we play Bible charades and Bible Pictionary. When the grown-ups sit around and talk, the kids practice Bible charades and then act them out to see if the parents can guess. They stop their talking and watch. We all have so much fun. When we play Bible Pictionary everyone draws a Bible picture on a separate sheet of paper, and then we guess what each other has drawn.

On special Sabbaths Mom and Dad take us to the nursing home where the old people live. We usually go with another family. The kids and parents sing songs. The kids say Bible memory verses. Then we all shake hands and pray with the people. Sometimes we'll go to a regular hospital to visit one of the church members who is sick. I feel happy when I am helping to make someone else happy. Sabbath is a special day to make others happy.

I never feel bored on Sabbath. Sabbath is special. There are so many things to do. I'm glad God made Sabbath for me.

Austin

This will be the last time for me to tell you how special Sabbath is to me. My sister Debbie told you about Sabbath traditions. The Sabbath tradition I like best is sundown worship.

When the sun goes down on Sabbath, wherever we are, or whatever we're doing, we stop to sing. We tell Bible stories. And we make a family prayer circle.

I feel happy at the end of the Sabbath. I'm happy because I had a special day with Jesus and my family.

Sometimes God gives me a special present at the end of a sunny Sabbath. He gives me a sunset. Sunsets are so pretty! The sky is dark blue way up high. The clouds are pink, orange, purple, and yellow. I think sunsets are God's way of telling me He had a special day with me. I know God likes to be with me on Sabbath.

I also feel sad at the end of the Sabbath. I am sad because Sabbath is over. Now I have to wait six more days until it will be Sabbath again. I really like Sabbath!

Our family always sings a sundown worship song called "Day Is Dying in the West." I asked Mom why we always sang that song. She told me that it was another Sabbath tradition. The words of the song talk about sunset and nighttime rest. The song also talks about the stars that shine at night. They are like little lamps in the sky. The song helps us to remember that God is holy. Mom says that holy means that something is the most special in all the world.

God is the most special. Sabbath is the most special day of the week. I am special too. God loves me. I love God. And I can't wait till next Sabbath.

My Special Sabbath Traditions...